How to Pick the Perfect Roommate

Volume 1
The Ultimate Roommate Guidebook Series

Michele Hall
and
Kathrin Lake

A What Works Media Publication
Vancouver, Canada

Cover Design Michele Hall
Michele Hall Photo by Olivia Fermi

For more information:
www.UltimateRoommateGuide.com

All rights reserved.
ISBN 978-0993608827

Copyright © 2015 by Michele Hall and Kathrin Lake

Dedication

This book is dedicated to my brother Jason who invited me to the West Coast to live with him in a remarkable home with some amazing and wonderful roommates who soon became longtime friends. As we went along the path of turning a ramshackle older house with disgruntled roommates into a gorgeous and happy shared home we picked up, invented and stumbled upon the guidelines, tips and agreements that you will find throughout the Ultimate Roommate Guidebook Series. I am grateful to him and to all my roommates over the years who have shown me friendship, better ways of doing things, how to amicably resolve conflicts and the joy of a lifestyle where we are able to live like millionaires no matter what our income is.

Table of Contents

Introduction 7

Chapter One: What Makes Us Experts 13

Chapter Two: A Cautionary Tale 15

Chapter Three: The 6 Steps to Picking A Roommate . 19

Chapter Four: Who Makes the Perfect Roommate? 21

Chapter Five: Step 1: Intend 29

Chapter Six: Step 2: Announce 41

Chapter Seven: Roommate Scams 53

Chapter Eight: Step 3: Interview 59

Chapter Nine: In Person Interview 67

Chapter Ten: Ultimate Interview Questions 79

The Ultimate Roommate Checklist: 101

Chapter Eleven: Step 4: Check 109

Chapter Twelve: Step 5: Choose 117

Chapter Thirteen: Step 6: Confirm 121

Chapter Fourteen: Welcoming Your New Roommate ...127

Chapter Fifteen: The Last Word (for a while)...........131

Other Books: In The Ultimate Roommate Guide Series .137

About the Authors: Michele Hall 143

Kathrin Lake...144

Introduction

Yes, it is possible to have perfect roommates. And no, it's not just the luck of the draw. In fact, you're already halfway there simply by picking up this little book. So, whether you are leaving home for the first time, heading off to college or are an empty nester looking to find companions and cover expenses, my intention in writing *The Ultimate Roommate Guidebook Series* is to share with you the tools, tips and insights my roommates and I discovered in more than 15 years of shared living.

You will learn how to attract the remarkable and supportive people who will become your roommates, companions and, ideally, lifelong friends. You will discover foundation rules that work best for groups of people living together and how to live like a millionaire even if you have a pauper's income. Each book in the series covers an essential aspect of roommate living, but I believe the one you are now reading may be the most important of them all. Why?

Because room mating—in my opinion—is more about great relationship building than it is about cost cutting. Which is why the wrong roommate will make your life a living hell, and the right one can become a friend for life.

Over the many years that I've lived in shared homes—often in some of the fanciest parts of town—people have constantly asked me, *"How do you make sure that the people you pick for roommates are the fantastic ones rather than those who are destined to drive you crazy BEFORE they move in!"*

Good question. And if you too are looking for the answer to that million-dollar question, then you've definitely come to the right place. Sad to say I've met lot of people who swear that their roommate experiences were so awful they will never go there again. What a shame! Because no matter how you cut it, a happy life

INTRODUCTION

has little to do with the things you have accumulated in life and everything to do with the people around you.

In essence, a roommate is someone who will become part of your new family. The last thing you want is to come home to drama all the time or to a chaotic, messy kitchen when you just want to put up your feet and chill. Of course if you really want to live with a biker gang who tromp around the house stoned out of their gourds and blasting the paint off the wall with loud music, be my guest. But chances are you are looking for an environment that allows you to study without distractions, or come home from work at the end of the day to find your home is as it should be: a safe and peaceful respite from the world.

That's why we insist that you pick roommates that understand the number one Ultimate Roommate Guide rule: YOUR HOME IS YOUR SANCTUARY, your private get-away-from-the-world place where at the end of the day, you feel safe and comfortable. Personally,

I can think of no sweeter way of living than to surround yourself with caring, supportive and fun people…in other words perfect roommates.

That doesn't mean you can't have some awesome parties and get togethers. Celebration is one of the great joys in life and I can't think of a better way of celebrating than with a great community you have created virtually out of thin air.

That being said, I am delighted to help you through the hurdles of picking the right roommate(s). In this book my co-author, Kathrin Lake, and myself will be sharing some tricks of the trade (the recruiting trade, thanks for asking) that will provide you with the very tools that professionals use to select and hire only the cream of the crop of all the candidates applying for a job. We'll show you how to use these same tools (and a bunch more) to ensure you get the perfect roommates for your home.

But what if you are moving into someone else's place? No problem, these same tools can be used to make sure that the person you move in with is the perfect roommate for you. After all, you must screen each other to ensure that you are compatible.

Personally, I believe that having roommates makes many things in life easier, not harder. They provide companionship, safety and make the care and maintenance of a large home so easy that it doesn't seem to be a chore at all (if you've ever owned a home you know what a weekend-gobbler maintenance can be). I realized that the book you are reading, *How to Pick the Perfect Roommate* needed to be the first book because once you find great roommates, then the rest is a relative snap.

Take my advice and honor yourself by setting yourself up for shared living success. And if you define success as being happy—and safe— then you're on the right track.

Chapter One

What Makes Us Experts In Shared Living?

As you read this book and others in the Ultimate Roommate Guidebook Series, you will hear me often refer to *The Mansion*. Although as a young child I lived in many shared homes when my parents lived with co-workers from the theater, it was at *The Mansion*, a 5000 sq. ft. heritage home in one of the wealthiest neighborhoods of Vancouver, Canada that became the inspiration for this series of books. The house was so much more than simply a cheap way to live. By living together, instead of each having dinky, little apartments, we had lavish personal spaces and lived like millionaires instead of the paupers our income tax returns showed us to be.

Each of the six roommates in the house had

their own room. And living in an older house, those rooms were huge compared to modern houses or downtown apartments. When you walked in the front door you would never guess that it was a shared home. One of our roommates had a great eye for decor and made sure that our common spaces were as sumptuous and beautiful as any of our neighboring millionaire's homes were. My brother lovingly tended to the gardens, and the rest of us did our part to keep the home beautiful and clean at all times. It could not have been more different than the roommate experiences we had when we first left home as young adults.

The Mansion also was known as a destination spot for the best parties in town as well as hosting gatherings known as "Sweet Talks" in our huge living room once a month inviting someone to share their adventures at Burning Man, screen an inspirational film or perform a small musical concert. This created community way beyond the walls of the house and meant that we had a list of interested potential roommates when, on the rare occasion, a vacancy came up.

My co-writer, Kathrin Lake, spent over a decade sharing her downtown apartment with a series of one roommate at a time until she said good-bye to room mating in order to welcome her new husband to move in with her. At first she used no more discretion in choosing a roommate than she had done back in her college days. With disastrous results! We may laugh when we look back at our roommate fiascos, but it sure isn't fun living with someone with two very different personalities and you're always on edge as to who is going to show up when you bump into them in the kitchen. Kathrin brings a unique perspective and the best roommate interviewing technique I have ever encountered. You can't go wrong if you follow her excellent interviewing techniques.

If you have questions, suggestions or want to share successes about your experience with shared living, we'd love to hear from you: authors@ultimateroommateguide.com

May you enjoy the journey of sharing your home and life with others, and may you always look back at your shared living home with affection. At the back of this book are links to a variety of tools, processes and templates that you can download, print and use to make the best decision you can: getting the most perfect roommate(s) you possibly can.

Chapter Two

A Cautionary Tale

Sarah is a performance artist and massage therapist who wanted to create a shared home. She knew she wanted to live in a large house that offered plenty of personal space for each person. She needed a separate room for her home-run business as well as a common area that would be large enough to run workshops or hold community gatherings.

She found the perfect place in a wealthy neighborhood and convinced the landlord that she was the ideal tenant although the rent was high above her income level. Undaunted, she set out to find housemates. For a period of time, the house was everything she wanted. It even became a destination home for some of the best parties in town with live bands and Sarah dancing Cirque du Soleil style from a silk cloth suspended from a ceiling beam of the two-story living room. But, after only five months she was forced to give notice and the house was disbanded. What went wrong?

Well, first of all Sarah didn't read this book (or the others in the series). If she had she would have known how to organize and run a shared home, what rules to set in place to guide everyone in harmonious living and been able to enjoy a great shared house that would have served her for years. Let's take a look at just some of the things that she didn't take into account.

1) First, she went against her own intuition about one of her new roommates. Her guts said, "No", but her bank account said, "Yes." Consequently, she ended up with a roommate from Hell.

2) She had no practical knowledge of what the local tenancy laws were, but the roommate from hell did. He went to the Tenant/Landlord department and told them that she was illegally running a business from her home. Because he

knew what the laws were and used them to his advantage, she was stuck with someone she couldn't evict.

3) When the roommate from hell notified the authorities, she now had the eyes of the law watching her. The neighborhood she lived in was designated as single family dwelling only, which caused tensions with the neighbors.

4) She had no written agreements with any of her roommates and had not even requested a damage deposit when they moved in. This left her vulnerable when someone left without notice or couldn't pay the rent.

5) Sarah had failed to calculate the actual costs of running a large, rambling house over the winter. Naturally, roommates had moved on and when the bills came in she almost went bankrupt with a whopping $4000 bill for utilities. As she was the sole leaseholder, she was fully responsible for these expenses.

My writing this book is in large part to help

others like Sarah to have fun and healthy room mating experiences. It's really very simple…if you follow a few simple guidelines.

Chapter Three

The 6 Steps to Picking A Roommate

It almost goes without saying that the most important "things" in your home are the people. The right people will make your shared home a welcoming and safe place to come back to at the end of your day. The wrong people will make your shared home a living hell. Many people new to shared living spend a lot of time finding the right place and fussing over obtaining the proper kitchen equipment, and then settle on the first person who shows up who can pay the rent.

My suggestion? Do the opposite:
- Don't rush into accepting just anyone as a roommate.
- Don't let finances rule the day.
- Make sure you've gone through the list of attributes that will ensure you are compatible.

Below are six simple, easy-to-follow steps to ensure you get a perfect (or near perfect) roommate.

Step 1: Intend - Imagining Your Perfect Roommate
Step 2: Announce - Posting Ads and Searching
Step 3: Interview – A Two-Part Interviewing Process
Step 4: Check - References, Personal, Business, etc.
Step 5: Choose - Pros and Cons, Gut Check
Step 6: Confirm - Sign an Agreement

In the following chapters we will go into greater detail on how to implement each of these steps. But before we do that, let's look at who makes a perfect roommate and who might not!

Chapter Four

Who Makes the Perfect Roommate?

Imagine staggering around the kitchen before dawn looking for your first mug of java. Do you still smile, 'Good Morning' as your roommate wanders in? Are you happy to see them or does their scowling face remind you that you wish you'd chosen better? A perfect roommate is simply someone whose presence is pleasant to be around. They are open to chatting about what works for them and what does not. They are willing to sit down and set up common agreements (or agree on the ones you already have in place). In short, your perfect roommate is someone who is easy for *you* to live with.

Now, how do you go about finding that person or persons? No, don't go racing to the closest roommate finder site (at least not just yet).

They often have elaborate lists to fill out in order to determine (electronically) if you are compatible. But before you do that, let's look at a few other things to consider.

What about relatives, lovers or friends as roommates?

You have a friend who is interested in moving into your place. You're already friends, so why would you go through the steps of interviewing them? It may seem like an obvious choice to move in with someone you know—after all you already get along. But beware! What was a good friendship can quickly turn sour if you find that you and your buddy have very different lifestyle habits. It's one thing to laugh it up when you go out to a party; it's quite another when you can't take a shower because your buddy in the next room used all the hot water in a massive laundry binge. Having to deal with the mundane details of daily life can take the zing out of just about any relationship if you are not careful.

Is your best friend always calling you for

romantic advice? Is there just way too much drama with emotional breakdowns every time she and her boyfriend have a fight? You already know this about her, so don't invite that into your house unless you love being the shoulder to cry on. She can still be your friend, but perhaps not your roommate.

Siblings & Other Relatives
The same rules apply (interview, discuss and sign an agreement) if you are considering moving in with siblings, cousins or other members of your family. You're probably pretty familiar with their lifestyle habits, but if you already know that something about them bugs you, then you need to address it up front. If your sister's habit of borrowing your clothes without asking drives you crazy, then you need to bring that up in an interview chat with her.

Tell her that an important rule for living together is that NO ONE TOUCHES OTHER PEOPLE'S BELONGINGS WITHOUT PERMISSION. Make sure she agrees and just isn't saying so for the sake of appeasing you.

Put it in your written agreement (it's number three of the basic Ultimate Roommate Guide Rules). If she truly understands that it's time to drop that childhood habit, then perhaps she has enough other qualities (other than availability) that make her a good live-in candidate.

I'm Thinking of Moving In With My Lover
Don't hold on to the fantasy that love will conquer all. Even if we saw firsthand how our own parents fought constantly over the tiniest things, we think that we can move in with our lover and it will be all sunshine and roses. Let me say it loud and clear: Breakups happen over the silliest things such as the "proper" way to squeeze a toothpaste tube. It's true! Look it up.

Which is why moving in with a boyfriend or girlfriend makes it even more (not less) important to set up guidelines in advance. For some reason, talking about house rules with a friend or a sweetheart can be more difficult than with a casual acquaintance or a complete stranger. It's sort of like talking about your favorite sex positions. It's suddenly extremely awkward! There seems to be an underlying assumption that if you demand guidelines from your lover then you don't trust them.

It's also harder to move out from living with a lover than a regular roommate. Once you move in together, you are essentially "hitched." Deciding to get a place on your own after living together is tantamount to getting a divorce. So, if you want to keep your romance alive, sit down and hammer out agreements in advance. In fact, this is so important I've dedicated an entire book to this subject called *The 7 Secrets to Setting Up House with Your Lover.*

For all the above reasons—and many more—be they friends, siblings or lovers, make sure you take each other through the interview process. *Oh God!* I hear you say. *I couldn't do that!* Really? Interviewing your lover about his/her lifestyle choices is a fantastic way to get to know them even more deeply. It's the perfect time to lay things out on the table. "I like to live like this...," or, "I need to have my home look like this...". Don't assume you can work things out later. NOW is the time to be clear. Habits that are endearing when you see someone a few times a week can turn toxic when you live with them every day.

That being said, the roommate experience is a great time for inner and outer growth. You will learn skills and behaviors that you did not expect. So be open to surprise. Your fussy friend may be the ideal person to inspire you to finally declutter and have your place looking lovely at all times. Maybe they have the right balancing energies to your lazy and crazy ways. This is where you definitely want to listen to your feelings (Step 5).

Finally, when it comes to choosing a roommate from your family, friends or current sweetie, don't let guilt sway you. Honestly, it's for the best of everyone concerned if you consciously CHOOSE your "new" family. Yes, of course that can include people you've known for a long time, but be realistic and honest. Follow steps three through six in the following chapters. Make sure you do a full interview to find out if you truly are compatible as housemates and not simply great hangout buddies. Take some time and listen to your gut instincts: "Does this feel right, or not?" And most importantly: SIGN AN AGREEMENT. Yup, I know. It's tricky. But if push comes to shove, tell them that *The Ultimate Roommate Guide* ladies say so. There, that should cover that awkward moment.

Chapter Five

Step 1: Intend

Just Who Are You Attracting?
Recently I had the opportunity to meet up with a woman who had posted on Facebook that she was looking to create a shared home and wanted to find others who would be interested in finding a place together. This is what she posted:

> *"OCCASIONALLY" MATURE, NON-SMOKING ROOMMATES WANTED*
> *I am an "occasionally" mature, non-smoking woman with a 16-year-old cat and a large collection of outdoor plants. I would like to find at least 2 two or 3 mature, non-smoking adults who are involved in personal and spiritual growth,*

to find a house together. I have a quite a bit of furniture so that's why I prefer a house. I like to grow my own fruit and veggies, too, so having a garden is very important to me. You would have to be willing to commit for a period of one year and take full responsibility for cleaning and maintaining the house and yard.

If you're "not into housework", please do not reply. I am not a clean freak, however, I am not willing or prepared to play "Mommy" to a house full of adults, either! Due to my cat being 16 years old, a small, obedience-trained dog that is used to being around cats, might be O.K. Another senior cat might be O.K. too.

If you're tired of spending most of your income on rent and would like to live in a truly nice, affordable "home" and you'd like to have some people to share your good times – AND! - Your bad times,

STEP 1: INTEND

please contact me ASAP so we can all get moved in before the monsoons! Thank you!

What she did right: she stated what she wanted: mature, non-smoking adults (although the "OCCASIONALLY" threw me. Did she mean she was pretending to be mature or that she thought mature sounded too boring?). She also made it clear that there would be a yearlong commitment. That's good. Then what stopped me in my tracks was her rant about not being a "Mommy" to a house full of adults. Whew! A little heavy-handed. Sounds like she's got some issues on this one.

Her ad is more of a turn off than a turn on. She sounds like a whiner, someone who finds faults and problems with everyone. In person, I asked her if she realized her ad was unlikely to attract the kind of people she wanted to live with. I suggested she put forward her vision of what she wanted and then have processes like proper interviewing processes, house rules, house meetings as well as communication and conflict-resolution tools for handling the inevitable upsets when the show up. This surprised her. And it may surprise you. You do not attract what you want by focusing on what you don't want. That's a bit like going into a restaurant and telling the waiter everything you DON'T want to eat, rather than simply letting them know what you do want.

Dr. Wayne Dyer says it perfectly, "You do not attract into your life what you want. You attract what you are." So if you are critical, picky and obsessive…beware! When you are looking to find the perfect roommate do the following:
1. Focus on the positive.
2. Interview fully, and
3. Learn to be flexible.

STEP 1: INTEND

Intending To Have Perfect Roommates
Pause for a moment right now. Close your eyes and imagine living with your new perfect roommate. See yourself sitting at the kitchen table chatting about your day or philosophizing about life. Imagine going on outings together. See yourself inviting friends over and everyone hanging out. Imagine the best possible situation: Someone whose company you enjoy, who is supportive to your needs and whose lifestyle and personal habits are endearing—or at worst amusing—rather than irritating.

This type of imagination is called visualization. It's a way of "calling in" your ideal roommate. Yeah, I know it sounds hocus pocus, but give it a try. It's astonishing how often what you picture in your mind comes into being when you make a conscious intention.

I am attracting a female roommate

> *who is fun to be around, but also enjoys her own company. She is clean and tidy and is easily able to pay the rent.*

Or:

> *My ideal roommate is a 30 something male who likes to go on long hikes with me on the weekends. He is funny and has great friends. We enjoy each other's company.*

From years of creating intentions I know that things usually work out when I intend them. This "intention" means I get to drop my natural tendency to worry. Instead I intend "that I will find the ideal roommates who will care for my house like it's their own while I am traveling for four months," or "I will find a female who is English-speaking," (I've had foreign students and that's fun, but sometimes it's tiresome to always be straining to communicate).

STEP 1: INTEND

Write down your intentions and post them on your fridge or mirror where they will continue to remind you subconsciously of your intentions.

Go For It:

Here comes the fun! Intention is most potent when you put it in writing. List the personality, qualities and values that you envisioned in the last exercise. To download the templates for this section, go to: www.ultimateroommateguide.com/picking

Print it up and use it as Step 1 in finding your perfect roommate.

> My Perfect Roommate is: *(list personal attributes like funny, classy, worldly, honest)*

HOW TO PICK THE PERFECT ROOMMATE

My Perfect Roommate likes to: *(list activities such as go out dancing, read, write poetry, play sports, go on long hikes)*

My Perfect Roommate is: *(list personal habits such as tidy, organized, casual)*

My Perfect Roommate can: *(list household duties such as garden, cook, paint, do accounting)*

STEP 1: INTEND

Now string them altogether and see if that sounds like someone you can see yourself living with. For example:

> *My perfect roommate is a mature thirty-something career woman who likes to work out. She is clean and respectful and cares for my place as if it's her own. She is great in the kitchen and occasionally we cook up a storm and throw together a dinner party for our friends.*

Naturally, you also have to take action. Post ads online at sites such as Craigslist; check out roommate finder search engines for your area and post on social media to let your friends know that you're looking. But, don't fret. Know that soon the magic will show up. Days might go by without a phone call. And then out of the blue, the phone starts to ring, and the emails start to pour in from perfectly suited candidates.

Great. Now let's be realistic. I know I said you were going to intend the perfect roommate, but life if nothing else is serendipitous. Having a roommate is like an exchange program. They will teach you new household tips, habits, attitudes and behaviors as well as learning new things from you.

At the Mansion, one of our roommates, Jimmy, had the habit of uttering the most politically incorrect statements. I usually sided with the other roommates, rolling my eyes whenever Jimmy spouted off. One day we were all in the kitchen and Jimmy said something so strange that we all just stood there aghast at his inappropriate blurtings. While we were trying to come up with a response, Annie went and gave Jimmy a big hug saying, "Oh Jimmy," in the most endearing tone. After that he changed completely and seemed to put more care into what he said. Annie showed us that

STEP 1: INTEND

sometimes all an awkward person needs is a bit of affection and acceptance.

So intend the perfect roommate...and then be open to the real human roommate who does show up.

Chapter Six

Step 2: Announce

One of the strangest things I've noticed about roommate ads is that people spend more time talking about the space than the face! Are you eating dinner with a space? Are you negotiating bathroom time with a room? Obviously not. Make your roommate ad stand out by telling people who you are, what kind of roommate you are looking for, what you expect and then—and only then—describe the space you have available.

But won't that turn off a lot of people? Maybe, but are they the roommates you want in the first place? The perfect roommate understands the necessity of good roommate selection and agreed upon living arrangements.

Where to Advertise

There are literally hundreds of specialized online roommate finding sites to help you both search and post ads for roommates. Some of them cost, some are free. Most offer options to filter for age, gender, photos, etc.

Viewing photos can give you a stronger sense of the person. It's even better if they have a good profile with hobbies and a list of likes and dislikes as this removes much of the guesswork. There are many good sites to post and search for roommates. Craigslist is probably the most popular in most countries. If you are looking for other sites, you can search for popular sites by country at: http://myaddsposting.blogspot.ca/

These online sites are usually best suited for large cities. A smaller town may not have enough people searching to make the use of such sites practical, though many smaller communities also have their own local sites.

STEP 2: ANNOUNCE

Let your friends know you are looking by posting a notice or a link to your ad on Facebook or other social media site. Often a friend knows someone who is looking for a place. Remember, a friend of a friend is still only a prospect. Do a proper interview and don't simply accept them without getting to know if they are really a proper candidate for your shared home.

Newspapers are virtually dead for roommate type ads, but many small towns publish community papers and carry want ads. Local YMCA's, libraries, gyms, colleges and even many workplaces usually have notice boards where you can pin up an ad. Make sure you get permission or you will be wasting your time if they remove postings that have not been properly cleared. Your ad can contain what you are looking for: gender, age range, professional or student, etc. If the place you want to share has great features, broadcast those loud and clear.

We have a working fireplace that is ideal for gathering around and sharing stories on a cool evening.

Have fun. Be poetic and who knows what wonderful people you will attract?

Be clear about exactly what have to offer and what you want, because believe me, people will ask you the dumbest things. If you say you have one room in a shared home, they will invariably ask how many rooms are available. Sigh! But be patient. They have probably looked at hundreds of ads and have lost track of who is who.

Do:
1. Post ATTRACTIVE photos of your place - common rooms, the room available, special features. Show pictures of the space AT ITS BEST. I'm constantly shocked at how people will go to the trouble of taking a photo of a bedroom, but

STEP 2: ANNOUNCE

not make the bed first. If you wish, post a photo of yourself. This really helps people decide if they like the impression they get from your photo. **Note:** make sure you do this in a safe way. You do not want to attract the wrong characters.

2. Describe your perfect roommate in a fun and interesting way: Do you like to hunker down on Sunday afternoon with a bowl of nachos and watch the game? Fancy having a beautiful garden filled with vegetables you grew yourself? The better the description, the more likely that the right person reading this will say, "That's me!"

3. Give your ad an interesting header or title.

4. Sell your place a bit. Does your apartment building have a pool and a gym? Is your place close to a shopping area? A subway? Libraries, banks, etc.? Maybe you have a great deck or a hot tub in your shared home.

5. Let people know what is included: all utilities, Wi-Fi, satellite TV with 150 channels, laundry room, etc. These all make your place more attractive (but remember you are also looking for compatibility over amenities).

6. Post in all places above, i.e. online, public community boards, a notice board in your building or where you work, and through social media ensuring friends and family are also helping with your search.

Knockout Criteria

We have already outlined some of the points to include in your ad, but let's look a little closer at some typical knockout criteria that may be important to you.

- **Sexual Preference.** No, this is not about theirs or your sexual or romantic habits. Often women want to only live with other women or sometimes gay men because of concerns about sexual harassment and

STEP 2: ANNOUNCE

safety. Unnecessary tension is a valid issue for them. Sometimes gay men only want to room with other gay men, ditto straight men. You have a right to ask for someone who matches your comfort zone.

- **No smoking.** If you are okay with some kinds of smoking and smokers, as long as it is done outside the house (stairs, porch, etc.), you can say that in your ad. HOWEVER, my experience is that people will often break rules when it comes to their addictions and habits. So, it's better to say a big fat NO unless you are a smoker yourself.
- **No drugs, no alcohol, no partying.** Most people will say "social drinkers" are okay, but many an alcoholic is in denial so you will also want to ask some more probing questions in the interview to find out for sure. Put it in the ad up front because those who like to party hard are likely to "de-select" themselves and not

even respond to your ad.
- **No meat or vegetarians only.** Some people cannot abide the smell or sight of cooked or raw meat and don't want to be around it or have it in their kitchens. That is their knockout.
- **Employed, professional or financially stable.** This is aimed at discovering their financial dependability. You will need to ask questions about finances, but some people will not answer your ad because they are unemployed. Putting easily verifiable criteria in your ad, such as their employment status, dramatically increases the likelihood of finding an employed and financially stable roommate.
- **Note:** Just because a person is not employed, does not mean they are not financially responsible. If they are self-employed, find out how long they have worked for themselves and how well that is going for them. Another note is that

STEP 2: ANNOUNCE

self-employed people often work from home and that may or may not work for you to have someone around the house all day.

- **Quiet/Sociable.** Often people advertise for the personality type that has worked for them in the past. Not that only these types will apply, but some people will de-select themselves if they feel they are not a fit. Be specific about what works and what does not work for you. For example, I knew a man who always advertised for "a person who enjoys dinner parties," because that was a big part of his life. It was very smart of him to state it up front and look for someone compatible. Many people would de-select themselves on that point alone, while others would be delighted to live with someone who has friends and a great social life.

Recently I found a great ad on a collective house network site that illustrates how to let others know who you are. As you can see, she shares a lot about more about her interests and her lifestyle choices that some people would be hesitant to announce. Yet, she has a better chance of getting what she's looking for simply by being very clear about what works and what does not for her.

I'm a female author with a strong mystical/spiritual bent who loves living with people. I enjoy my privacy, and equally enjoy cooking together, playing board games and discussing books and politics. I'm an environmentalist and love all animals, tame and wild. I do not have a pet, but would be very happy to live in a house with yours.

I divide my time being out and about doing performances and readings at festivals/libraries, going to concerts and volunteering with therapeutic riding/animal

STEP 2: ANNOUNCE

rescue, and working on my computer.

A nonsmoking house is essential, as I have 7 years of recovery from nicotine, and am highly allergic. That means no "social" smoking, no smoking outdoors. I'd prefer a room on the main floor. I'm omnivorous and a wicked cook with a popular Ukrainian cookbook. I use cruelty free, nontoxic cleaning products and cosmetics.

I enjoy living with people from widely diverse backgrounds. I march in land claim and civil rights rallies, and rarely missed a "Take Back the Night" march.

I play piano and sing, and would be bringing my electric piano. I use headphones if necessary for others' quiet time. I recycle conscientiously and notice when the garbage needs to be taken out. I'd like to live with people who discuss house chores, are clear on household expenses, and will also take the initiative without having a meeting for every detail. I believe most people can manage themselves, and don't need micromanaging.

I'd appreciate a home close to a rec center and a park. I swim four days a week and enjoy walks. I look forward to hearing what you have to offer.

Now there's a gal who understands that to be in the right house, you need to clearly state what you want and who you are. You may have already spotted some things that are knockouts for you, but for others they would be saying, "Hey, that's my perfect roommate." Because, in the end a knockout is simply something that absolutely DOES NOT work for you.

Chapter Seven

Roommate Scams

Fear, Uncertainty and Doubt
While 98% of the people in the world are good and honest, occasionally there are hucksters who will try just about anything to get a few bucks. One of the worst fears of placing online ads is that you will meet unsavory characters, criminals, or worse. Naturally it's important to exercise caution when you invite strangers into your home. If you are a single woman, you may want to have a friend over when you interview male candidates.

There is also the possibility of being the target for a common tenancy scam that costs roommate seekers to lose money every day. Sites like Craigslist, Kijiji, and even legitimate roommate search sites, are ideal places for those scammers who constantly troll for the gullible.

How the Scam Works

You receive an email from a potential roommate interested in renting your room. They tell you that they are a stable, reliable person who is moving to your city and looking for a place to live. They give you a story about how they just got a job nearby or they are going to school. So far, it sounds legit. They then tell you they cannot meet with you in person because they are overseas or there's not enough time before move-in day.

Somewhere in the exchange of e-mails, they say they will send you the total amount of the rent plus the security deposit to secure the room. Be wary of any email from someone who is eager to finalize payment on a place they've never seen, let alone the fact that they've never met you. This is where you need to pay attention! When you get an email like this, just stop all communication.

Back before this scam was well known my roommate Ron, who was managing *The Mansion*, almost fell for it. What alerted him to the fact that something was fishy was that the emailer said she was moving to Vancouver to pursue a modeling career. Unbeknownst to her, Ron had been a male fashion model and knew that Vancouver was far too small to have full time modeling jobs. However, he didn't smell a rat yet and waited to see what would unfold. He accepted her offer to pay two months' rent in advance (the amount will vary, but will always be enough to bait you). The scammer then mailed a check or international money order. It looked authentic.

Even the bank did not immediately detect a problem. Thankfully in this case, banks are notoriously slow in cashing overseas checks. As soon as Ron confirmed to the emailer (another warning sign) that he had deposited the money, the scammer twisted the knot a bit tighter. Another email from the "model" informed him that she had to cancel moving to Vancouver as her grandmother had just died. Would he please take something to cover the inconvenience and send her a money order for the balance?

What's wrong with that, you may ask? Well, it turns out that her check was a forgery and eventually the bank declined the funds. If Ron had allowed his heart to win, "Poor girl. Such a shame about a death in the family just as she was pursuing her career," then he would have sent her a legitimate check (or international money order) that she would be able to cash. Ron would be out of pocket, not to mention losing another month's rent by having no one to move into the house. It's a clever way that foreign scammers can get your money.

An even more sophisticated scam exists where you meet in person and see the space. They act as though they are the property managers when they have simply rented the space themselves. They con you by offering a discount if you pay for six months in advance. Of course when you show up with all your furniture it turns out that the apartment or house belongs to someone else entirely. Now you are out of pocket AND homeless!

The Simplest Way of Not Falling for These Scams:

Protect yourself by finding out what the local rulings state about rent deposits. Usually it's one month or one and a half month's in advance. And **NEVER, EVER** rent to someone you have not met in person! Simple. If you don't meet them in person, you can't do the in-depth interview process that we recommend to ensure you get your perfect roommate. So, let's get down to that right now.

Chapter Eight

Step 3: Interview

For many years my co-writer, Kathrin Lake had a job as a recruiter and HR professional. She was trained to ask questions and to listen for the warning signs that a particular candidate was *not* right for the position. In fact, she discovered that when she listened people would inadvertently tell her things about themselves that immediately knocked them out of the running. This is the skill we want you to discover. Listen carefully to what a potential roommate shares with you, because your future happiness with your perfect roommate, or your misery with the roommate from hell is hidden in their responses to the questions we will be giving you.

For about ten years Kathrin had roommates in her lovely downtown Vancouver apartment. As she will tell you, she used to pick some doozies: sociopaths and neurotics who almost made her regret having roommates at all. Then one day the obvious smacked her over the head, but let's allow Kathrin to tell you in her own words what she did.

Kathrin Lake

Interviewing and Interviewing Questions

As an HR professional, I had extensive training in the best practices for hiring top candidates and have successfully placed hundreds of people in great jobs with top companies.

Around the same time it made sense to upgrade my living situation to a gorgeous, two-bedroom suite downtown that cut my commute down to

STEP 3: INTERVIEW

ten minutes. I realized that the best way to be able to afford this new place was to get a roommate. I had not had a roommate since college days and I don't remember doing much interviewing then. So, I selected a roommate the same way I did back then (which was pretty cursory). Enter my own "Roommates from Hell": an abusive, compulsive liar, a closet drinker, and a completely dependent and financially broke individual, to name just a few of the crazies I was bumping into in the kitchen or on the way to the bathroom on a daily basis.

Ironically, every day as a recruiter I went to great lengths to interview and select only the best and most qualified candidates for the very prestigious and picky companies I worked for.

I finally woke up one day and asked myself, "Why wasn't I applying the same skills I used in my job to ensure that I only got the best roommates possible?"

So, I crafted a series of very specific selection questions and interviewed prospective roommates using the same techniques I did in my recruiting job. Once I had refined it, I was hard-core inflexible about this process. Voila! My next three roommates were delightful, each staying about two to three years, and remain to this day amongst my closest friends. I am now living with my husband, who I trust is my last roommate.

Key Areas for Questioning
The underlying wisdom for choosing a perfect candidate is that "past behavior is the best indicator of future behavior." This means you need to find out as much as you can about your candidate's past and do it as quickly and thoroughly as possible.

The prime areas you need to focus on to find out as much as you can about a potential roommate are:

1. Financial dependability
2. General accountability
3. Flexibility and compromise
4. Emotional maturity

STEP 3: INTERVIEW

5. Ability to communicate
6. Conflict resolution skills
7. Work schedule
8. Smoking, Drugs and Alcohol habits
9. Domestic habits
10. Sleeping habits
11. Bathroom habits
12. Cooking and food habits
13. TV watching habits
14. Music playing habits
15. Friends and family habits
16. Romantic or sexual habits
17. Hobbies
18. Furniture and "Stuff" volume
19. Household tastes
20. General personality

Yikes! That looks overwhelming. How can you manage all that in an interview, you are undoubtedly asking yourself. The quick answer is: you can't. However, in as short as ten or fifteen minutes on the phone you can find enough out about them to determine if they have triggered one of your knockouts by asking them questions in your "most important" areas.

The Phone Interview

Don't for a second think that people will read the ad carefully and apply because they mentally checked off all your boxes. You will need to ask them again about what you already stated in your ad. The sad truth is, people do not read ads, and certainly not carefully. If they have a Great Dane and you are allergic to dogs this is obviously not a match.

Before you meet them in person, inform them about your preferences with: *"I don't know if you noticed what I am looking for, but are you a non-smoker, vegetarian, and a professional woman?"* You will be flabbergasted how many will answer "No." If I had $5 for every time a man answered an ad that requested in bold letters "WOMEN ONLY," I would have made my rent money many times over.

And don't forget the criteria set out in your building rules that also need to be considered in the equation. A typical one is NO PETS, or CATS ONLY. Most people have a clear feeling about pets in particular, or are bound by

STEP 3: INTERVIEW

building rules. DON'T LET ANYONE OVERSTEP THE BOUNDS OF YOUR TENANCY RULES. It doesn't matter how cute the puppy is, or how temporary you were told its stay is going to be. Be firm now to avoid situations down the road that can get you in hot water with your landlord.

After the right answers to the knockout criteria are confirmed by phone, invite potential roommates to see your place and have a face-to-face to determine if they like it (and you). You ALWAYS want to meet them in person for the final interview.

Chapter Nine

In Person Interview

Now, let's walk through the most effective way of conducting an in-person interview. I'm going to show you the same interviewing skills I was trained to employ as a professional recruiter and then went on to apply to great success in selecting the best roommates I've ever had. This, I will repeat, was after years of horrible roommates using the "sure-whatever" approach I had used back in college. Of course I've softened my original recruiter tactics as potential roommates are not expecting to be given the third degree. If you push too hard, or repeat questions they have already answered, they are likely to flee.

As a corporate recruiter, our candidates expected us to make them jump through hoops by asking them very challenging and probing questions. It's quite another matter when you interview a potential roommate. Don't do the full police interrogation on them or you will scare them away. Stay focused, but at the same time keep it light and conversational. It took me awhile to fine-tune the adjustments of my interviewing technique. What you most want to do is put your candidate at ease and make them feel as comfortable as possible.

I would always invite them to sit down at the kitchen table and play host offering coffee, tea or water. I would then invite them to ask any and all relevant questions they want of me first. A good roommate situation is a two way street. By setting the right tone at the outset you are preparing for open and healthy conversations about housekeeping and management in the future. If they never asked me any questions at all, then it was an immediate red flag.

Nonetheless, as anyone in the business of interviewing will tell you, the key to getting the answers you want is *to ask the right questions*. In a casual conversation you want to find out how easy they will be to live with. Part and parcel of this process is a technique called *Story Prompting*. By using stories, you are employing the human love of gossip to probe a little deeper and find out how they previously responded to similar roommate situations.

Open-Ended Questions
First, what are open-ended questions? These are questions that cannot be answered with a simple yes, no or a one-word answer. In other words, they require a longer response. Why do you want to use them? To elicit actual stories and to gather more information about what actually happened under those

circumstances. This is the opposite of them simply telling you what they think you want to hear.

By prompting them to give longer responses, and use their memory of actual events, it makes it harder for them to make things up on the spot. Plus, it fulfills what studies have confirmed: "past behavior is the best indicator of future behavior." Great open-ended questions will give you clear insight into their past behavior.

The Sandwich Technique
A simple interviewing technique will help you probe deeper to discover if your potential candidate is, or is not, a finalist for your perfect new roommate.

Not all your questions will be open-ended. When and how you ask open-ended questions is important. You want to move from soft, easy questions to middle questions to hard-

IN-PERSON INTERVIEW

hitting questions. You want to ease into the harder questions gradually. This is called *The Sandwich Technique* and consists of putting a hard-hitting question between two easy soft questions. Imagine the hard-hitting question as the meat of what you really want to discover. You cushion that tough question between easy, soft questions that are the fluffy white bread of your sandwich.

Unlike a corporate interview where the candidates mostly ask their own questions at the end, in a more personal kitchen or café situation, it's more of a back and forth dialogue while still getting all the information needed. Which is where story prompting comes in.

Story Prompting
When you use open-ended questions you prompt your potential roommate to recall their own stories of past events. Do this in a conversational way by sharing your stories

first. This strengthens trust, allowing them to relax and be themselves. Believe me, you will find out a whole lot more when they are relaxed with this method than any other way.

Here is an example of an open-ended story prompt to find out about the "financial dependability" of your potential roommate (number one on our list of the 20 things you want to know about).

> STORY YOU TELL: *Every month I use my computer to make sure I get my bills paid on time. How do you manage your bill paying?*
>
> When they have answered how they manage their bill paying, you then use secondary questions to follow-up or "probe." This ensures you have the information you really need.

> PROBE: *Do you get everything paid on time every month that way?*

Remember, you want a lot of good information without being too hard fisted. Be genuinely curious and interested, which you should be if you are going to live with them. It keeps it conversational when you've just shared a story or a bit of information about yourself. The example stories below are simply suggestions and fall back ideas. Make the questions and stories your own and definitely don't overtly lie about what you are saying. Lying is not a good way to start out any relationship.

Let's go through the questions that we have found work for each of the 20 elements, and label them soft, middle, or hard. Some will be simple and some will be more in depth. Don't be embarrassed to ask the harder questions. You will avoid a lot of pain later on if you find what you need to know up front. So, now's the time.

One of the most amazing parts of being a recruiter (and later applying these techniques to roommate finding) was how easily people will share things about themselves that obviously put them out of the running if you ask the right kind of questions. Here are just a few responses that resulted in me silently REJECTING candidates as roommates:
- "Yes, I play guitar and have to practice regularly. Sometimes electric and sometimes acoustic... How often? Day or night. Whenever the feeling moves me."
- "I only smoke when I drink and I hardly ever drink. Only in clubs and on the weekends and when others are around."
- "I expect my sister and some of my family might be staying over... Oh, only once every three weeks or so.

And only for three or four days at a time I expect."
- "I'm not very mature."
- "My boyfriend might be staying over. He's looking for a job, so it's hard for him right now, and he's struggling with his rent, but he's a great guy. Would that be okay?"
- "I have a job… reading tarot cards… part-time… My Employment Insurance ran out but my relatives said they have something lined up for me… What? I'm not sure. When? I'm not sure."
- "Yes, I have bounced a check before. Hasn't everyone? But hardly ever… maybe only once a year."

As you can see, people have different ideas about what is "too much" or what is not a big deal for them. The right probing questions will reveal what your prospect's "norms" are. Thankfully there will also be people who *are* on the same page as you in the areas that are most important to you.

Remember, a simple chit-chat will NOT give you the insights into their character that you need to determine if they will make a perfect roommate or not. Ask questions from the 20 keys areas we have outlined and don't be afraid to probe more deeply using the Sandwich Technique. The last thing you want is to discover you don't really know who they are until they have the keys and have moved in.

Download and print up the Interview Questions as well as the **Ultimate Cheat Sheet** to have on hand for your interviews. Print up one for each person you meet in person. Fill out the basic information - name, phone number, email, references, etc. but DON'T fill in their responses until after your candidate has gone.

Do fill it in as soon as possible after they've left as it can get darn confusing trying to remember who was who when they are not in front of you.

Chapter Ten

Ultimate Interview Questions

As you read through these sample questions you may notice where some areas cross over with others. You won't have to use all of these, but you should probably use at least ten. Make sure you find out the information that is most important to you, whether it is around financially dependability or domestic habits, and stay alert for whatever triggers your personal knockouts. Don't be shy; just keep being sincerely curious and interested. Remember the **Ultimate Interview Questions** are the full version, but you may want to have the **Ultimate Cheat sheet** nearby to help prompt you as to which questions to ask. These are both available as downloads at: www.ultimateroommateguide.com/picking

1. **Financial Dependability**

Soft – *Where do you work? How long have you worked there? Do you like it?*

Middle – ex: STORY TO TELL: *I use my computer to make sure I get my bills paid on time every month. How do you manage your bill paying?* PROBE: *Do you get everything paid on time every month that way?*

Hard – *Have you ever bounced a check before? (Any check, not just rent checks).* PROBES: *How often does that happen? What happened last time? When was that?*

2. **General Accountability**

Middle – *Some people are always 10 minutes early, 10 minutes late or always on time? Which are you?*

Note: Were they late for meeting up with you? If so, what excuse did they give and were they sincerely apologetic?

Middle – STORY TO TELL: *I once had an ex-partner who said I was responsible enough for both of us. What would the people closest to you say about your ability to be responsible?* PROBE: *Why do you think they say that? What do they see*

you doing for them to say that about you?
Hard – *Have you ever left any rented places without giving full notice? Why? What were the circumstances?*

3. Flexibility and Compromise
Soft – *How flexible are you generally?*
Middle – ex: STORY TO TELL: *I had to compromise with my last roommate about when to have shower and bath times. I agreed to start taking my showers in the evening instead of the morning. Have you ever had to compromise on something like that with someone you lived with? PROBES: What was it? Were you okay with the compromise?*
Hard –*When have you ever refused to compromise on something a past roommate asked for? OR Have you ever had a roommate refuse to compromise on something you wanted? PROBES: What was it? What happened? Did it work out okay between you?*

4. Emotional Maturity
Soft – *Who was your best roommate? PROBES: What made them a best roommate*

for you? How long did you live with them? Will they give you a reference?

Middle – *What was your worst roommate experience? Why was that? On what terms did you part from former roommates? Good? Some good, some bad?* PROBE: *What happened in the case of the bad ones?*

Hard – ex: STORY TO TELL: *There was a time I was upset with my roommate because she dropped a candle, started a fire, which we put out, but it scorched the rug. Can you think of something careless that a roommate did that upset you like that? What was it?* PROBES: *What did you say? How was it handled? Was there yelling?*

Note: Even though there's a tendency to make the other person the one at fault, you can tell a lot about your interviewee by listening to how they frame the issue.

5. Ability to Communicate

Soft – *How do you like to communicate; what's your communication style like?*

Middle/Hard – ex: STORY TO TELL: *I had a roommate who never told me ahead when she* *was having her boyfriend over, or when she was staying out late, even though I asked her to just give me a head's up. Was there ever a roommate that you thought had poor communication skills?* PROBE: *What did you do about him/her?*

6. Conflict Resolution Skills
Soft – *Are you a person who likes to handle conflicts head on? Or, do you tend to avoid conflict?*
Middle – ex: STORY TO TELL: *I had a roommate who got very upset at me because I would sometimes forget to lock the door and I had to set up a system to remind myself. Have you ever had a roommate give you some feedback of something that upset them?* PROBES: *What was it? How did you respond to them? How did it get settled?*
Hard – *Has anyone described you as passive aggressive before? Has anyone suggested you don't handle conflict well?*
Note: Be very careful with people who get really aggressive or defensive about these hard-hitting questions, it is a big flag, not just for a

roommate but also for the rest of the interview. Keep it soft and polite for the rest of interview and get them out, or get out of there and decline them later... on the phone.

7. Work Schedule

Soft – *What's your work schedule like? Do you need to get up early? Do you work night shifts? The answers to these questions will also determine whether you have to tiptoe around at night or if there is a conflict with bathroom times in the morning.*

Middle – *How often do your work hours change?*

Hard – ex: STORY TO TELL: *I had a roommate who worked from home but liked to work all night and sleep all day, so I felt like I was tip-toeing around during the day and couldn't make any noise. Have you ever had an issue like that where your work schedule clashed with someone else's?* PROBE: *How did you deal with that?*

ALWAYS ask how *did* they deal with something as opposed to how *would* they. We want to know past experiences not ideals. It is tempting to slip back and let them say what they would do instead of what they *did* do. Make sure you keep it on track and ask about the *actual* past.

8. <u>Smoking, Drugs and Alcohol Habits</u>

Often this will be a follow-up for your knock out questions, but good to address again.

Soft – *Remind me again, did you say you were a social drinker? A non-smoker?*

Middle – ex: *In your past shared households what were the policies around ... smoking... alcohol...mild drugs... partying?* PROBE: *What happened at parties? Did you sometimes partake?*

Hard – *Are there any drug habits you have, I should know about now?* IF THIS COMES UP PROBE: *How long have you been clean and sober?* You need to determine your comfort level of accepting a person in recovery. Generally I would not want to live with anyone who has fewer than two to five years clean and sober in recovery and has passed all other requirements. Also, if I am a drinker or mild drug user, and there will always be temptations for this person around, I would PROBE: *Is it your criteria to be in a clean and sober environment?* If they say it doesn't matter without a good explanation, you can wonder why not. That's a flag.

9. Domestic Habits

Soft – *What are your pet peeves around housekeeping?*

Middle – *How did you get on the same page with housekeeping with former housemates?*

Hard – *Looking around at how I keep my house, would you say you are cleaner than me, about the same, or that I am cleaner than you?*

PROBES: *How have you resolved differences in domestic habits in the past? What were the big issues?*

Note: If you are interviewing in your own space, don't clean it up as if your mother was coming, but keep it at "average" or its neutral cleaning state and let them know this, to see how they react. You won't be able to hide it later, so don't hide it now.

10. Sleeping Habits

Soft – *What time do you generally go to bed at night and get up in the morning?*

Middle/Hard – ex: STORY TO TELL: *I had a roommate once who snored so loudly I could hear him through two walls. Do you snore or walk in your sleep, or have any habits that I should be aware of?* PROBES: *Have you ever had to live with someone who was loud at night? How did you handle it?*

11. Bathroom Habits

Soft – Do you prefer a shower or a bath? Morning or night?

Soft – What are your pet peeves about how the bathroom is kept?

Middle – How often do you usually hang clothes in the bathroom? How did you share spaces in the bathroom?

Hard – ex: STORY TO TELL: *We had a policy in my college household that we would leave the toilet bowl clean, and light a scented candle if needed, for the next person, except at night when we were allowed not to flush, both to be more green and so we wouldn't wake anyone. What* *are your habits around flushing the toilet?* **PROBE:** *Do you flush every time? How do you prefer to deodorize?*

Note: If this question embarrasses you, or you are afraid it may frighten away a roommate candidate, don't use it, but it's good to clear up embarrassing issues early on rather than having to bring them up later.

12. Cooking and Food Habits

Soft – *What are your pet peeves in the kitchen or things you cannot tolerate around cooking? Do you like cooking? Do you enjoy shared meals?*

Middle – *How did you manage a shared kitchen in the past so there were no disagreements?* **PROBES:** *What kind of issues came up in the past? How did you resolve them?*

Hard – ex: STORY TO TELL: *I had a roommate who would eat my food and not replace it. I had to have a talk with her, more than once. Have you ever had that kind of situation before?* PROBE: *How did you resolve it?*

Hard – ex: STORY TO TELL: *My past disagreements around the kitchen seem to be around loading and unloading the dishwasher and when you are allowed, and not allowed, to leave dishes in the sink? What do you think the rules should be?* PROBE: *How flexible are you on those rules?*

Please feel free to come up with your own soft, middle, hard questions on the following topics (or others you might have):

13. TV Watching / Game Playing Habits
Adjust questions to address gaming as serious gamers can take over a living space with loud and violent games that never seem to end. If this is not your thing, finding out now is the way to avoid tensions down the road.

Soft – What *programs do you like to watch on TV?* (Not a bad break the ice and personality compatibility question too). Do you play Nintendo or other video games?

Middle – *Do you watch a lot of TV/play video games?* PROBE: *How important is it to you? How many hours a day? Which shows are a must see?*

Hard – ex: STORY TO TELL: *I had a roommate who never told me they disliked my TV show habits until it came out in a flare up. We had to work it out.* PROBE: *Have you ever had any TV disagreements like that with roommates before? Are you willing to pay for a hook-up in your own room?*

14. Music Playing Habits

This can be recorded music or instrument playing from someone who is musically inclined.

Soft – *What kind of music do you like to play?*

Middle – *Do you play a musical instrument?* PROBE: *How often do you practice? Has this ever been an issue with people you have lived with?*

Hard – ex: STORY TO TELL: *In the past there were different ideas of what were acceptable music volumes, tastes and what hours you could play music, so we sat down and made some agreements.* PROBE: *Have you ever had issues around music before? What guidelines worked for you in the past? What is important to you around music?*

15. Friends And Family Habits

Soft – *Do you have family and friends in this*

area? Just be social and ask more about them.

Middle – *How often do you see your friends and family now?* PROBES: *Do any of them like to drop by? How frequently?*

Hard – ex: STORY YOU TELL: *My parents usually come to stay in my room for couple of days once a year and I sleep on the couch. Is that okay?* PROBES: *How often do your out of town friends and family stay with you for overnight visits? How often did they visit last year?*

16. Romantic Habits

Soft/Middle – *Are you romantically involved with anyone at the moment?* PROBE: *Will you be staying at their place sometimes? How often will they stay here?*

Hard – ex: STORY TO TELL: *We had one past roommate who was into online dating, but it was more like online hook-ups, and I was very uncomfortable with strangers in the apartment.* PROBE: *How often do you think you might have love-interests over? Is there a way you have handled this in the past in order to make sure your roommates feels comfortable and secure?*

Note: You may want to set limits to number of nights a lover can stay over, before they end up as unofficial live-ins. Make it clear that they can't just slide from a night or two into full time live-in. This is a serious area of contention and needs to be agreed before hand or dealt with quickly when it comes up. See *Rules for Roommates (you know you need 'em)* for more information.

17. Furniture and "Stuff" Volume

Soft – *How much furniture and other stuff do you have?* PROBE: *Will you need additional storage?*

Middle – *Do you have furniture for the common areas that you wouldn't want to live without?*

Hard – ex: STORY TO TELL: *Often the way we have handled double items in the past, like two toasters or two couches, is to determine who has the newest or most compatible stuff and put the doubles in storage if possible. But sometimes there are still conflicts, people don't want their things touched, or there's not enough room in storage. How have you handled* *such things in the past?* PROBE: *How do you think we should resolve any conflicts so there isn't too much stuff in the common areas?*

18. <u>Hobbies</u>

This is more of a break the ice, personality and compatibility question. Unless the hobby is likely to impact other roommates or the space, you don't need to probe.

Soft – What do you do on your time off (recreation, hobbies, friends)? PROBE: *Has your _____ ever bothered any of your roommates or neighbors?*

19. <u>Household Tastes</u>

Often, one person can see your tastes by looking around the place, but you don't see theirs so this is where you may have to ask and refer to your own suite.

Soft – What *style is your furniture?*

Middle – *This is our style and décor taste. Is it compatible with yours?*

Hard – ex: STORY TO TELL: *I once had a shared roommate situation where we were allowed to say if one object in the shared space* *bothered us that we could ask our roommate to keep it in their own room. That's how we resolved taste clashes. I'm not sure it was a good idea or not but... How have you resolved differences in taste in the past?* **PROBE:** *Did you have any concerns? Do you have concerns now?*

20. <u>General Personality</u>

Obviously you are looking for people who like living with others. Find out if the reason they want a roommate is based solely on cutting costs. If it is, then they are probably not the happiest roommate you'll ever have.

My personal choice is that I don't really like living alone. I hate coming home and saying, "Hi, I'm home!" to the houseplants. I like people in my home. So if that is not so for you, ask yourself if you need to change your perspective and fully embrace the spirit of shared accommodation.

Middle – ex: TO SHARE: *My past roommates would say I am a pretty laid-back person, how would your past roommates describe you?*

You may want to be wary if they say very little to this question, or are not sure how others view them.

REMINDER: If they have never had previous roommates, many of these questions may seem not applicable. In this case ask them about their family situation. Everyone has lived with someone before, so many of these questions can also apply to siblings or family).

Hard – *If you had a choice would you prefer to live alone or with good roommates? PROBES: What do you like most about living with others? What do you like least?*

Sample Exchange of the Sandwich Technique & Probe Techniques:

(Hard questions sandwiched between some softer questions, plus gentle probes to find out more)

> YOU: What style is your furniture?
> CANDIDATE: A lot of Ikea, and a couple of antiques my Mom gave me.
> YOU: I probably have that too. Looking around at how I keep my home now, would you say you are cleaner than me, about the same, or I may be cleaner than you?

CANDIDATE: (looks around) About the same.
YOU: That's good, but what are your pet peeves in housekeeping? I like the kitchen counters clear for example.
CANDIDATE: I like a clean bathroom and bathtub.

YOU: Was that an issue in the past with any past roommates?
CANDIDATE: Oh yeah.

YOU: What happened?
CANDIDATE: I finally had to tell my roommate that I needed him to clean out the bathtub every time after he used it.

YOU: How did he react?
CANDIDATE: He was surprised. He didn't seem to notice. He did clean it after that, mostly.

YOU: So when there is a domestic conflict, do you tend to handle it straight on, or avoid it?
CANDIDATE: A little of both I guess

(laughs nervously)
YOU: *Did you leave on good terms with your bathtub roommate?*
CANDIDATE: *Mostly. I don't really speak to him anymore.*
YOU: *Do you prefer shower or bath?*

What did we learn from this exchange?
- Our décor and household tastes may be the same.
- We probably have similar domestic standards.
- This person has a big pet peeve in the bathtub area.
- This person may be the type to hold onto their issues and then later ambush someone.
- They may not be someone who handles things straight up.

Later on, if I were still seriously considering this person I might throw in a question like: *Has anyone ever called you passive aggressive before?* Just to be sure. Before you start thinking, *I couldn't ask that*, you should know that I once did ask that of a roommate candidate. Her answer to my probing question was: *I used to have that tendency, but I'm now aware of it and working hard to change that behavior.* Because we had a thorough interview and were clear from the start, we got along very well as housemates. She is now one of my dearest friends.

Making Notes

You might wonder, with all these questions and answers, should I be making notes while we are talking? This is tricky because you don't want people to be uncomfortable. They may not open up if you jot all their answers down while you are interviewing them. My best answer is: try to write very few during the interview. However, write as many as you like right after the interview of everything you can remember. If they are an immediate knock out, then just jot down a quick note why. You will want to review your notes after interviewing a few candidates because it can be easy to get them mixed up after a time. If there are two top candidates, looking back at your notes to see how they responded will push one person ahead of the other.

During the interview, it is all right if you note only pertinent information like where they work, references, previous roommate or landlord names, contact information, and verifiable things you may want to check on. When you do start scribbling, apologize to them and tell them you have a terrible memory for details, even if you don't, just to put them more at ease.

Download and print up the **Ultimate Interview Checklist** to have on hand for your interviews. This will help you may your interview guest more at ease:
www.ultimateroommateguide.com/picking

The Ultimate Interview Checklist

When you are the one interviewing the roommate:

- ☐ **Small Talk** - Use something to break the ice, the weather, their commute in, where they grew up, anything that can be considered small talk and non-threatening. Find some common ground and build rapport.
- ☐ **A Beverage** – After they see the apartment (if you are showing yours), have them sit down with you over a tea, coffee or water in the suite. If you are intending on looking for a place together, or it is not your place, ask if they can sit down with you in their place or meet in a café (not in a bar). If they will not sit down with you, or it is hard to get them to agree to that or schedule

it, consider that your first flag.
- **Ask some Easy Open Questions.** After small talk, start with some easy and obvious questions. Only do the hard ones after sharing some stories or when you are sure the person is at ease. Pause between each question and allow them to ask things too. Be prepared to answer their questions, and keep it conversational but remember you have an agenda to find out about this person.
- **Be Adaptable** – Make the questions your own and be prepared to make up questions on the fly that you think would be good for this person and whatever they are saying or doing. See probing further.
- **Share Your Stories** -- If you don't have any roommate experiences, use living with your family as examples. When you share, they open up to sharing with you. It is a matter of trust. You will find that the answers will come faster and better if they feel you have opened up too. You also get to observe their

reactions as you talk to them. Are they looking concerned when you tell them that you had problems with a roommate that always had their friends over? If so, ask them about that.

- ☐ **Prompt Stories.** Ask them outright, "What are some of your roommate experiences around... cleaning, music playing, bathroom sharing, cooking, etc....?
- ☐ **Be Curious.** When they tell stories, ask for what actually happened in detail in these examples. This is what we call in the recruitment biz, 'Behavioral Interviewing'. Use How, Why and What follow-up questions and be curious..."What did you say to them?", "How did you respond to that?", "How did you work that out?", "How did that end?" or "Why did you do it that way?"
- ☐ **Ask Hard Questions After Easy Soft Questions.** When you are sure the person is at ease, ex: you just asked what they like on TV, you can now ask some of the hard hitting questions, like,

"Have you ever bounced a check before?" Observe how they react when you ask hard-hitting questions. How quickly do they answer? With how much confidence? What is their expression?

- ☐ **Request References** - If they find it strange you are asking for references, tell them that you have learned the hard way, or that you made a promise to your building manager/family/other housemates, etc. to do this and you promise to be polite and discreet to their references.

- ☐ **Close Friendly–** Make sure you end on a friendly note even if you know you are crossing them off your list. Let them know you are still interviewing. AND if you think they are on your shortlist, show your enthusiasm for them. BUT don't tell them they are "the one." Tell them you need to check references and you will make a decision by... (give them a time that you can get back to them).

THE ULTIMATE INTERVIEW CHECKLIST

If You Are Being Interviewed:

- ☐ **Be presentable,** dress comfortably but avoid being either too dressy or too dumpy.
- ☐ **Bring reference list.** Bring these but do not bombard the interviewer with them unless they are asked for.
- ☐ **Small Talk** - use something to break the ice, the weather, your commute in, and a person who you may have in common. Find some common ground and build rapport.
- ☐ **Beverage and Sit Down** - If coffee, tea or water or nothing but a seat are offered, do accept and be prepared to stay for a time and find out as much as you can.
- ☐ **Prepare Answers** to the questions that we gave you in advance. Have five or so key stories or examples of past experiences that show you are reasonable, responsible and flexible and also get them talking too. Unless you are not reasonable, responsible and flexible in some area, then be honest what your

weak spots are, and how you are going to be aware or manage them.
- **Can't Think Of A Good Answer?** – Be honest. If you have no great answer to their question, say you unsure about that and tell them why you are unsure if you can. If it seems like an odd question they are asking, it is okay to ask them why they want to know that. Then, listen to their answer before you judge and then decide if it is appropriate to answer.
- **Don't Get Defensive!** Do not try to read into questions that they are trying to imply something, just respond courteously and if the questions seem inappropriate, ask them why they want to know. **If it is really uncomfortable, make a quick exit.** "I am sorry I have another appointment," works well.
- **Be Prepared With Your Own Questions.** Have a list of five or more critical questions that you want to know more about. You should be thinking of things as you go along as well. You can't ask too many questions, after all

you are considering living with this person.
- [ ] **Money & Time.** Make sure you get your money and timeline questions answered before you leave: "May I call you on Thursday?" or "Can you let me know by Saturday as I need to make a final decision soon."
- [ ] **Close Friendly** – Get any contact information and final details sorted and make sure you try to follow their lead to their way of saying goodbye. If they just say goodbye, do that too, or if they shake hands, do so as well. If they bow, do so. If they hug, also do so, and note that this person may be more physically comfortable right away, and if you are okay with that, fine, otherwise realize this may be a challenging person for you.
- [ ] **Note**: When shaking hands, make sure you match their energy in their handshake, not too soft, or too firm.

Chapter Eleven

Step 4: Check

Red Flags and Green Lights
Let's have a look at some typical Red Flags that say, "Don't pick this person," as well as some Green Lights that tell you, "This person is a straight shooter".

Red Flags
1. They are very late for the interview and their excuse is not plausible and they don't seem too concerned about it.
2. They are in a hurry and don't want to sit down and talk.
3. They bring a friend or family member who seems more enthusiastic than they are about them moving in with you.
4. It is an acquaintance or friend of a friend and since they think this person is a good egg, you don't feel you have to do a full

interview process with them. Don't fall for that. I did once in college and voila: psycho lady.

5. They look like hell. This is a tricky one and you should get to know them a little first before you totally judge the book by its cover. You need to ensure you are not projecting petty prejudices, but if they really look slovenly, and it is not just fashion tastes you are seeing, consider how it may reflect on their domestic habits. Also, it can indicate they are a bit of a party animal and were out the night before ... but it could also mean they pulled an all-nighter at work. Find out!

6. You feel like you are selling yourself and the place too hard. This is a flag for you against you. If you hear yourself wanting this person too much, realize that you may be under the influence of what we call "the halo effect." A seemingly perfect person walks in the door and you decide right away they are "the one," so much that it blinds you to the fact that they are not responding well to you or

STEP 4: CHECK

your questions. Beware!

7. They seem overly concerned about one thing, such as, their commute in, how far they are away from their current love-interest, etc. You want someone fully enthusiastic about both you and the place.

8. Someone who hesitates during the financial dependability questions. When they were relaxed, I liked to ask the question: *Have you ever bounced a check?* If they hesitated in answering, "No" right away, I simply didn't take them on. You see, my best roommates, who are still friends, are the ones who said "No" immediately.

9. Someone unwilling to give you an appropriate deposit in cash. Be firm about this, even if everything else in the interview went well. This could definitely spell future money troubles. Be ready to axe them and go to number two if they are not getting it together. Remember the maxim: How you do one thing is how you do everything.

10. They ask you strange or overly intimate questions that are not really pertinent to living together.
11. They are overtly gloomy or admit they are suffering from depression or mental illness. Not to stigmatize those individuals, but it's essential that you guard out for your future happiness, and seriously consider this as a flag.
12. They don't ask you very many questions at all. You want a roommate who is as caring and concerned as you are, so if they ask a bunch of questions that is a good thing. Rarely is there a candidate who asks too many questions.
13. They are pushy and want to move in right away, disregarding your approval process.
14. They are aggressive or defensive when asked some questions or told there is an agreement they need to sign.
15. They talk too much or too little.
16. Your gut says, "No".

Green Lights

1. They answer your financial dependability questions without hesitation.
2. They show a genuine enthusiasm for you, the place, its location and any of your co-roommates.
3. They ask you as many good and pertinent questions about you, how you handle things and the living situation.
4. They have shown a lighter side, or sense of humor. They don't have to be an extrovert or social butterfly, but just a general sense that they are a happy, reasonable person.
5. You have a chance to see their current living place and can see that their domestic habits and tastes are compatible with yours.
6. They seem to be appropriately open and don't mind your questions at all.
7. They are polite, considerate, on time, and helpful.
8. They are clean, well groomed and healthy.
9. They are prepared, know what they are

looking for, when they can move, and that they have a cash deposit ready.
10. They neither talk too little, nor dominate the conversation, but seem to have an appropriate sense of when to speak and for how long.
11. They have some ambitions, recreations and/or hobbies in their life.
12. They don't mind looking at and signing an agreement.
13. They enjoy living with others and say so.
14. Your gut says, "Yes".

Reference Checks

Ask your candidates for a variety of people as references: former roommates (best choice), a landlord, an employer and personal friends. Ask them to inform their references that you will be calling. Naturally, they will be giving you references from people they are pretty sure will praise them. This is understandable. However, don't be afraid to ask some tough questions to their references about your roommate candidate. Be wary if a former roommate or the current landlord seems to be overly enthusiastic

STEP 4: CHECK

and gushing superlatives about your candidate. It may be that they are desperate to get them out of their own place quickly and see you as helping them do that.

If none of their references return your calls that may also be a flag. Check back with your candidate to make sure they have given you the correct contact information. Sometimes a candidate is new to town and has no local references.

Two of my best ever roommates were cousins who had just moved to town. In fact, I was interviewing them not as roommates, but as temporary tenants who would sub-lease my apartment for four months while I travelled. The only local reference they were able to provide was their employer and of course all he could say was that they had been employed by him for a couple of weeks. Not a lot to go on. But they were very personable and likable young men. I had a good gut feeling about them. They turned out to be perfect care takers of my place, even going the extra mile by having the carpets cleaned just before I returned and having a vase of flowers waiting for me when I got home. Not something I expected from two 20-something guys.

Chapter Twelve

Step 5: Choose

If, in the end, you've gone through the whole process and you're still not sure, do a check-in with your gut. Instinct is ignored far too often. Yet, it's often that "funny" feeling that is saying "No" even when everything else seems to be okay.

In an earlier chapter I told you about Sarah who set up a large shared home in a fancy part of town, but soon ran into trouble. The rent was very expensive and so instead of listening to her gut feeling, she over-rode her instinct to disastrous effect. Her new roommate turned out to be very manipulative and confrontational. He was determined that her massage business was a cover up for "other" activities and at one point climbed up a ladder to peer into her treatment room when she had a client.

Despite involving the police, she could not get him to leave until he had received his thirty-day notice. It created a lot of tension and bad feeling in the house. I'll never forget Sarah telling me later, "I knew there was something I didn't feel right about, but all his credentials were fine, so I didn't listen to my gut feeling."

Now is the time to go over your notes and memories of what was said in the interview. Is there something that seemed a bit odd? Remember that past behavior is the best indicator of future behavior. So if they seemed overly critical of former roommates, for example, watch out as you're likely to be the next "horrible" roommate they complain about.

We once invited a friend of a friend to move into our big shared home. She told us a sad tale of how she needed to move out of her former place as the person downstairs was "poisoning" her with chemicals he used in his dark room. Although my ears perked up when she told her story (who uses a dark room anymore?), I let this detail pass and she moved in. Soon it became evident that it wasn't other people who were poisoning her, but her active imagination. Her bedroom was armed with massive, expensive air cleaners that were so loud I had trouble sleeping even across the hall from her.

She claimed that people were sneaking into her room and moving or stealing her things and then putting them back a few days later...just to mess with her head. She carried her purse over her arm even to make a meal as she was convinced that people were stealing her money. Eventually it became very clear why she never stayed long in any one place.

So, if you've asked the right questions, listen to your intuition about that person. They will have given clear indications of whether they are right for you or not. You just need to check in with your intuition and/or ask your other roommates how they "feel" about the potential new roommate. You'll be happy you did.

Chapter Thirteen

Step 6: Confirm

We may laugh at Sheldon on *The Big Bang Theory* and his multiple page roommate agreement, but being clear on what works and what does not work for you is essential for your own happiness. Comfort and safety are integral parts of the process of living with other people.

Far too many miserable roommate experiences could easily have been avoided if they had simply taken the time to be clear and upfront about their living arrangements. Unfortunately few people take the time and effort to discuss the terms or to sit down and write a contract or a set of agreements.

Do not fall for that trap!
Make sure you are protected by insisting on a proper tenancy contract when you move in

anywhere or when new roommates move in with you. Contracts and agreements are similar in that they are terms of interacting with each other that are clear and WRITTEN OUT. Contracts cover the terms of tenancy, money, utilities, etc. Agreements are the way you live with each other and can be hashed out between you and your roommate. Agreements cover the details of living together such as: kitchen duties, shower times, overnight guests, etc. These tend to be ongoing and should be agreed upon together at house meetings.

What is most important about a contract or an agreement is that the basics are laid out in black and white. There is less likelihood for confusion or misinterpretation when you can go back and review the terms on paper. This is such a big topic that I have written a whole book on the subject: *Rules for Roommates (You Know You Need 'Em)*.

Contracts

Whenever you move into a house, rent an apartment, accept a roommate or become

STEP 6: CONFIRM

someone else's roommate, make sure you have a written contract covering the details of your tenancy that is signed and dated by ALL parties. This is for the protection of EVERYONE. It's all too easy after the fact to say, "But I thought my rent included all utilities and this apartment doesn't have cable." A proper rental contract will have space for each of the utilities to be ticked off if they are included in the rent. If they are not, then it is up to you to provide and pay for those services yourself.

Have a blank contract form available when you interview a potential roommate. You can fill it in and sign it on the spot or give it to them to look over. The contract should indicate amount of damage deposit (usually one half to a full month's rent depending on the laws or the norm in your jurisdiction). If you have a big shared house that you are managing by yourself, you still need to ask for a damage deposit from an incoming roommate. It is your protection against unpaid rent or damage to the property. Remember you are ultimately responsible for these to your landlord. Many people with roommates fail to get deposits and then are left high and dry having to fork out the difference themselves.

Terms Of Tenancy
Your contract should clearly outline the terms of your tenancy arrangement stating beginning date of the contract, the duration (yearly, monthly) and how much notice is required by either party for termination.

It should also clearly state the amount received as damage deposit and the terms of returning that money. In most cases one month's written notice is required to terminate your tenancy. That does not mean that you can give notice on August 2nd for a September 1st departure. Be fair with your roommates and give them plenty of time to find a replacement roommate. In the above scenario your roommate could technically say you owe rent until October 1st.

To clarify, a contract:
- Is legally binding

STEP 6: CONFIRM

- Is between a landlord and a renter, or a primary leaser and roommates
- Defines the terms of tenancy including deposit, termination notice, utilities, etc.

Agreements

An agreement is less formal, but in many ways much more important. People moving in together often overlook this simple step. Agreements do not necessarily have to be signed but they should be written out. It's a good idea to post these agreements in a common area like the kitchen outlining what was decided by all at the last house meeting.

Agreements can cover:
- Housekeeping and house participation duties
- Common areas
- Noise levels
- Shower or laundry times
- Overnight guests
- Etc.

As mentioned, I go into a lot more detail in my book *Rules for Roommates (you know you need 'em)*. This book will really help you set up the rules and guidelines that will make your shared living experience fun, friendly and harmonious for everyone.

Chapter Fourteen

Welcoming Your New Roommate

You've gone through the process of posting ads, you've met a couple of suitable candidates and after careful reflection you picked what you trust will be your next perfect roommate. The contracts and agreements have been signed, money has passed hands. Now comes one of the most overlooked aspects of room mating: welcoming your new roommate. Chances are that they are moving into your place, a space that has been your home for a while. It's your shower curtain in the bathroom, your dishes in the cupboards and your couch and TV in the living room. While it's home for you, your "staking your claim" everywhere can easily make a new roommate feel like they don't belong. So what to do?

Remember there will be a period of transition for both of you as you adapt to the kitchen/bathroom dance and maneuver around each other's habits. Relax and have a welcoming attitude. A sense of humor also greatly helps.

The best thing you can do at this point is to go out of your way to make your new roommate welcome into what will now also be there home. Make sure that the whole apartment or house is cleaned to the level you like it to be kept at. This is an important message. If your new roomie sees dishes piled in the sink, then the assumption is that dishes in the sink are okay. If that is not how you want to live, then make sure it is up to your day-to-day standards when they move in. They are far more likely to keep it to those standards now that they are there.

It really doesn't take a lot to make your new roommate feel comfortable and at home. If a former roommate has recently vacated the room the newbie will be moving into make sure it is clean. Vacuum, dust and make sure that the light bulbs work and that there are plenty of hangers in the closet. Going the extra mile is a great way to make your roommate feel welcome. It could be a vase of fresh cut flowers in the room or a home cooked meal for your first dinner together (a nice touch even if you are not planning on sharing meals). Lend a hand in moving boxes or setting up shelves. At the very least offer some tea or coffee and a friendly chat in the kitchen when everything is moved in.

These small gestures create the self-fulfilling prophecy: you will be creating your perfect roommate by being a perfect roommate yourself.

Chapter Fifteen

The Last Word (for a while)

We trust you've discovered just about everything you need to know—and how to go about it—to get great (dare we say PERFECT) roommates. Don't forget to use the whole 6-Step Process. It may seem longer than simply going by your gut, but believe me you DON'T want to end up living with the roommate from Hell. Download and use the templates we have created for you to beat the odds and get roommates that are compatible, fun and easy to live with. And make sure you all sign a dated contract that outlines the terms of the tenancy.

Personally I believe that shared living is the wave of the future as more and more people come together to create new family constellations and community. Finding the perfect roommates is just the first step—though an essential one—on the journey of living a happy and conflict-free life with roommates.

Once you and your perfect roommate have signed a tenancy contract and agreed on a few basic roommate rules you will find that a number of other issues show up. One of the biggies is the whole area of how to resolve differences revolving around housekeeping and maintenance issues. Don't ruin your roommate relationship over trivial issues. And don't start WWIII over who scrubs out the bathtub.

I have several upcoming books that I recommend as the next steps in perfect roommate living: *Rules for Roommates (you know you need 'em)* and *Setting Up Your Shared Home*. These two books are chock-a-block full of great suggestions to ensure your shared living experience is tension free. They include some excellent tried and true conflict resolution techniques that not only get to the heart of the problem, but also help you build a better relationship with your roommates. These are great transferrable skills that will serve when dealing with challenges from lovers, co-workers or family members. I highly recommend that you add these books to your library and employ these easy-to-implement techniques in all aspects of your life.

The Ultimate Roommate Guide Series has been a dream of mine for a long time. I'm delighted to finally get this first book out. Thanks so much for reading it. And thanks to my co-writer Kathrin Lake for her unique perspective and fantastic interview techniques and questions. I trust they will help you get your perfect roommate.

What we'd love most from you is…feedback. Please post a review on the website you purchased it from. And we'd also appreciate hearing your personal room mating stories. Do you have a funny situation or a story of how you and your roommates worked out your difficulties? Love to hear them. Best of all, we adore hearing how people have created successful and happy shared homes. Email us

anytime with your stories, thoughts and feedback. We'd love to include some of them on the Ultimate Roommate Guide blog:
email: authors@ultimateroommateguide.com

Now go forth and enjoy your roommate experiences.

Templates

To download the templates for this book, go to:

www.ultimateroommateguide.com/picking

Perfect Roommate Intention Exercise

Interview Template

Interview Cheat Sheet

Sample Tenancy Contract

Basic Roommate Agreements

Other Books

In The Ultimate Roommate Guide Series

If you are looking for more support in the whole area of shared living, I have several other great guides to help you along the road to creating the perfect shared home.

If you would like to be informed when a new book comes out and receive some free tips on room mating, please sign up at:
www.UltimateRoommateGuide.com

Coming Soon:
Rules for Roommates (you know you need 'em)
This fun book is an absolute must if you have a roommate. Whether it's just two of you or you have a whole house of roommates this will help

you set up the right kind of boundaries. Like the proverb says: good fences make good neighbors. Good fences in this case are the rules (or agreements) that you and your roommates define so life in your shared home runs smoothly.

Shared Living for Grownups

Whether you are recently single looking for a place to lay your head while you heal your heart or are a retiree needing financial and other help in your home, this book will show you how this phase in your life can be the best ever…with roommates. While you may not have considered having roommates since you were in college, it is a very do-able alternative, lifestyle choice that can provide you with everything you need in life: luxury, ease, companionship and safety to name but a few of the many benefits and perks of shared living.

Setting Up Your Shared Home

Run your home at a profit! With that radical idea this book provides an outline for setting up

OTHER BOOKS

a shared home that is a beautiful home for everyone. Whether you are looking to invite people into your home as housemates or finding a house together, this book puts together some fascinating ways you can live like kings and queens even if your income is that of a pauper.

7 Steps to Setting Up House with Your Lover
Love will conquer all, correct? Wrong! While love is the mesmerizing force that brings us together, things can quickly sour when sweethearts decide to set up house. This book looks at simple ways you can keep the love in the relationship even when the dishes need to be done and the kitty litter must be emptied. Do yourself a favor: Before you make the leap to move in with your sweetheart sit down together and read this very important book.

Resolving Roommate Tensions
This is an essential guide to resolving conflicts. Whether it's the small daily upsets in housekeeping or lifestyle differences or more major breakdowns, this book is filled with tools to have your home be harmonious again.

How to Live with Relatives
Once upon a time the extended family was the norm. Not so much these days. Whether you have grown up children who just never seem to move on or it's time that your elderly parents moved in with you, this book will help set up guidelines in that trickiest of situations: living with family.

How to Pick the Perfect Tenants
You want tenants that not just respect your property, but treat it as though it were their own. Using similar techniques to picking roommates, this book focuses on the best tools that every small landlord should use to ensure they get the best tenants possible.

The Landlord's Guide to Shared Living
Does the idea of a bunch of people living in your rental home fill you with dread? Do you imagine wild parties where your income property gets trashed? This book shows you how shared living is the wave of the future and how you can ride this wave to increase the value of your home.

OTHER BOOKS

The New Family - Shared Living for Single Parents

Bringing up kids as a single parent is hard work. Why not create community and share the joys of raising children together? In this book we look at tools and guidelines that will mean kids are surrounded by the love they require and single parents get the support they so desperately need.

About the Authors

Michele Hall

With a long career in theater, television, film and radio Michele has fine-tuned the art of transforming rough ideas into interesting, captivating stories. Author, ghostwriter and book coach, Michele's recent books are *The One Minute Goddess, Bus Tales: How to Change the World from 9 to 5* and the *Ultimate Roommate Guide* series.

Michele loves living in community and shares a house with several wonderful roommates in Vancouver, Canada.

www.UltimateRoommateGuide.com
www.WhatWorksMedia.ca

Kathrin Lake

Kathrin Lake is former CHRP (Certified Human Resources Professional) with an interesting background as an award-winning playwright, newspaper editor, speaker and author. She uses Story Coaching to teach individuals and organizations how to use the "Power of Story" to create inspiration, clarity, and unity in a workplace. Kathrin founded The Vancouver School of Writing and is a full time writer, writing coach and organizes events to give training in writing and publishing both online and off.

Her first non-fiction book was "From Survival to Thrival", then "Putting Fear in Reverse Gear", "The A to Zen of Writing" book series, and "Writing with Cold Feet." She frequently holds seminars or gives keynotes about writing and publishing across The United States, Canada and Mexico.

www.kathrinlake.com
www.vancouverschoolofwriting.com

www.ingramcontent.com/pod-product-compliance
Lightning Source LLC
Chambersburg PA
CBHW061440040426
42450CB00007B/1147